SECOND BLOOM

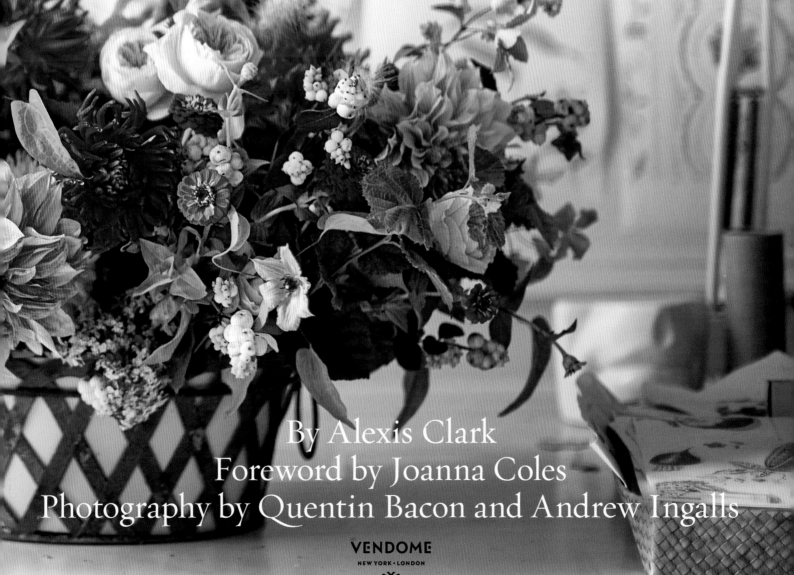

SECOND BLOOM
Cathy Graham's Art of the Table

By Alexis Clark
Foreword by Joanna Coles
Photography by Quentin Bacon and Andrew Ingalls

VENDOME
NEW YORK · LONDON

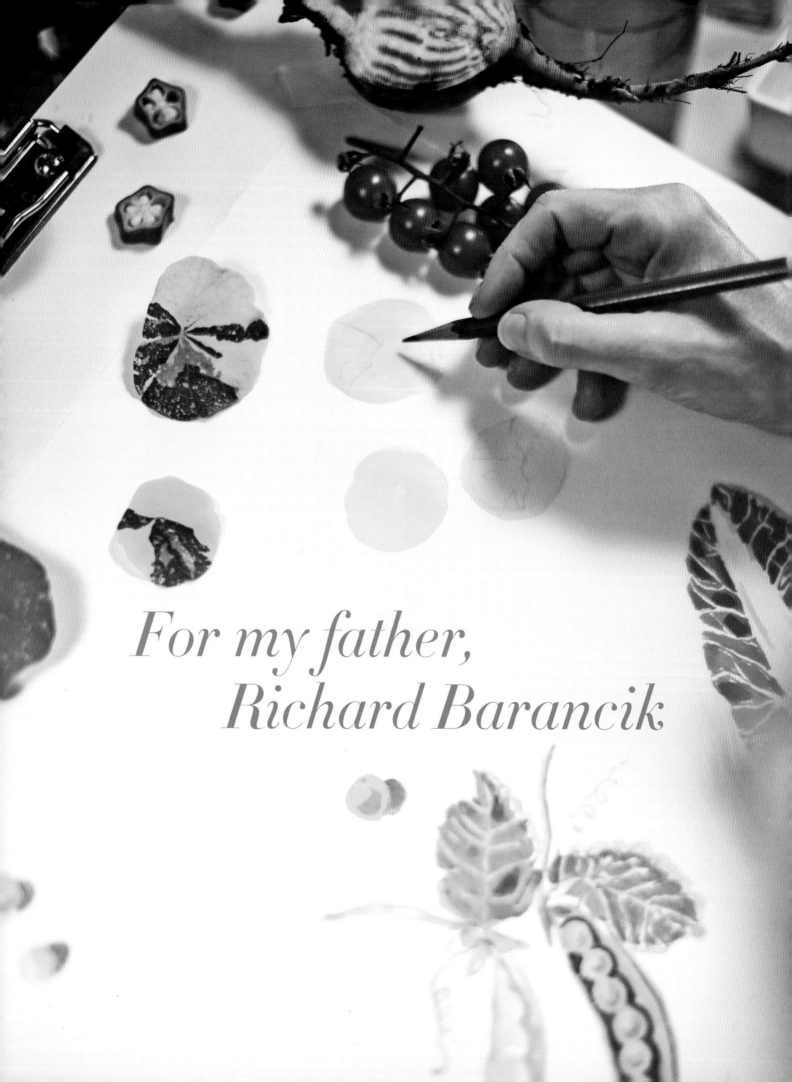

For my father,
Richard Barancik

For Alexandra

All The Best

Cathy Graham

Foreword

Oh what fun it is to receive an invitation from Cathy Graham. An envelope arrives. By hand, of course, because it wouldn't remotely fit into the standard Manhattan mailbox. It's not quite a square, it's not quite a rectangle, it's a strange parallelogram, an enchanting handmade envelope, sometimes tied with stripy string, and the handwriting of the address—in thick red or sometimes maroon pencil—is angular, specific, urgent. Impossible to be ignored.

Huzzah! The heart beats faster, for once you have wrestled the invitation from its paper cavern, there is always the promise of cocktails, or a party, or better yet, a special dinner, and there is always a reason to celebrate. An author's new title, an artist's latest exhibition, a designer's new stage set, a playwright's new production.

In the age of the evite, Cathy's handmade invitations are themselves works of art as individual as the artist being celebrated. There might be beading, a delicate whisper of fabric or raw white wool, fresh from the farm and fashioned into a woman's hair, as for the invitation to celebrate Flora Fraser's *The Unruly Queen: The Life of Queen Caroline*. Or perhaps there's a tiny doll's limb glued to the card, with a pressed feather or a circle of gauze, fluttery as a butterfly's wing, comprising a crazy collage to celebrate the range of William Ivey Long's extraordinary career as a costume designer. *Hairspray*, *The Producers*, *Crazy for You*— tiny nods to his achievements are not just scattered across the invitation but extend to the table and the mantel inside Cathy's soothing townhouse. Who else but Cathy Graham would go to the trouble of dressing doll mannequins in the costumes Long made for the characters in *Grey Gardens*, Edie Bouvier Beale and her mother, Edith?

And then there's the dinner table itself. No one can create a floral landscape like Cathy Graham. Forget the perfected, color-coordinated arrangements ferried in vans across the city from the latest celebrity florist. Cathy's designs have a wild charm that makes her table unique. Each stem is assigned its own vase, each blossom allowed its own spotlight. In the summer, picked each morning from her garden in Nantucket, there are pale roses blushing in tiny glass jars, fragrant stock flowers in antique medicine bottles, solitary dahlias and tall lilies standing sentry on the sideboard, and fat peonies in little fishbowls bursting their petal bodices. Yellow and white daisies jostle with single blue hydrangea globes and little glass test tubes of svelte lavender.

JAN 19th
ISAbella
BLOW
DAY 3

DAY 9
ELIANE
BONabeL
JAN 25th

DAY 13
CARA'S
DOG
JAN 29

DAY 15
JEAN SAINT-Martin
JAN 31

DAY 21
Feb 6

DAY 23
Feb 8

DAY 26

Feb 12
DAY 27

Feb 13
DAY 28

In fall and winter, the roses may be white, mixed with pansies, black-eyed anemones, chrysanthemums, tulips, and always, hidden among the flowers, quirky details that reflect Cathy's own dark whimsy as an artist. A child's small, abandoned doll from the fifties, tiny toy cans of peas and corn, little courtesy soaps from hotels glamorous in the forties but now gone bankrupt. A puppet's head, severed from its body, a miniature truck. Quirky details hiding among the perfect blossoms—with just a trace of menace. Only after sitting down do we notice above us an extensive mobile of baby turnips, pale vegetable moons with purple tails, spinning silently and suspended, brilliantly, from the ceiling by invisible fishing line.

An artisanal invitation . . . a magnificent tabletop . . . and yet the real reason to savor dinner at Cathy's is her unerring ability to make everyone feel at ease. As Andre Bishop, artistic director of Lincoln Center Theater and a regular guest, points out: "She gives all her guests equal amounts of her attention. And she is very tolerant of her guests' eccentricities. For example, they can't eat this or they have to arrive late or leave early or wear bizarre outfits or too casual outfits."

Like the best directors, she understands people, their appetites and timing. The canapés and cocktails in the drawing room last half an hour, so you're neither too full for dinner nor yet talked out. The move to the dining room is smooth—no chatty laggards holding everyone else up. A name card in Cathy's familiar handwriting greets each guest, and the seating is thoughtful—an old friend to the right, perhaps a new one to the left. Never bread, but to start perhaps a light risotto with a ruffle of truffle, followed by slow-cooked lamb or short ribs and a light chocolate soufflé. French-sized portions, no seconds—what a relief!—and always a quick welcome speech, frisked with grace and humor.

This is home entertaining at its best and most elegantly relaxed. Daisy the blonde Labrador may wander by, grazing for scraps, or a marmalade cat may saunter out, unhurried, from under a chair. And all the while the evening progresses. The burble of conversation is punctuated with laughter, earnest and then louder political debate, animated entreaties to read this or go see that, and the love of friendship and gossip.

And then all too soon the silver jugs of decaf appear, the bowl of crystallized ginger, the trays of sobering water, and the realization that normal life, so perfectly held at bay for three hours, is about to be resumed. Cathy's magical night is coming to an end. And there is nothing to be done except wait until the next one.

—*Joanna Coles*

Introduction

It doesn't matter the occasion—a festive cocktail party, alfresco luncheon, or formal seated dinner—step one foot into Cathy Graham's Upper East Side townhouse or summer house in Nantucket, and the flowers, tabletops, and frankly, just about every surface reveal that someone with sublime taste, a feminine color palette, and a love for ever-so-subtle hints of playful kookiness is your hostess. Trained as a painter and professional illustrator, Cathy has revived her artistic pursuits, to the delight of anyone who has ever seen her watercolors, her invitations, and, of course, her festive table settings and floral arrangements. Now in her very own *Second Bloom*, with two teenage children and newly single after years of marriage, she is embracing the return to her former career as an illustrator—the reason that brought her to New York in the first place so many years ago—and unleashing her passion for creating beauty with an infusion of her eclectic and vibrant personal touches.

Cathy's sometimes delicate and sometimes lavish but always fanciful and romantic aesthetic is perhaps best summed up by the words of the legendary floral decorator Constance Spry, fittingly one of her sources of inspiration. "Do what you please. . . . Just be natural and lighthearted and pretty and simple and overflowing and general and baroque and bare and austere and stylized and wild and daring and conservative. . . . Open your mind to every form of beauty."

And that's exactly what Cathy does each and every time she sits down in her sunlit studio to sketch, imagine, and lose herself for hours doing what she loves.

Art has been a part of Cathy's life since her early childhood in Chicago. Her mother, a painter, and her father, illustrious architect Richard Barancik, always encouraged her to pursue her love of drawing and painting. "From the time I could walk," she recalls, "we went to the galleries on Saturdays and the Art Institute of Chicago on Sundays. My lifelong love of miniatures began the moment I first saw the remarkable Thorne Miniature Rooms at the Art Institute."

Cathy went on to receive a BFA in painting from the Rhode Island School of Design, followed by courses in fashion illustration at Parsons in Manhattan. Some years later, at her mother-in-law's stunning seventieth birthday party, she met the late event designer

11

Robert Isabell, who had planned the extraordinary affair. It wasn't long before she went to work for Isabell, whom she refers to as a "visual genius," and they became best friends.

Cathy's style is undeniably elegant and sophisticated, yet sprinkled with unexpected elements. Who says a bouquet filled with variegated roses, tulips, and camellias, preferably in hues of pink, coral, lavender, and yellow, isn't perfectly accented with fresh herbs, kale, radishes, twigs, and cherries? Whatever is in season is what sparks her creativity, and nothing gives her more pleasure than finding the most colorful and structurally appealing flowers and fruits to display on a table or inspire her to paint.

For most of the year, when Cathy is in New York—fall, winter, and spring—the Union Square Greenmarket and the Flower District are her go-to purveyors for the lushest blooms. But during the summer, she steps right outside the front door of her Nantucket beach house into her treasured garden.

The philosopher Cicero said, "If you have a garden and a library, you have everything you need." Cathy has both, and she spends as many hours curled up with a book as she does picking and pruning in her yard. An oasis, refuge, and source of creativity, her cutting garden is where she connects with nature and immerses herself in rows of hydrangeas, dahlias, clematis, sweet peas, foxgloves, and poppies—the very botanicals she may combine in a centerpiece or garland, or display individually in the vintage glass bottles she's been collecting for years.

Whatever she finds inspirational is what she picks, which doesn't limit her only to flowers. The fruits of her labor, quite literally, can also be turned into beautiful arrangements. Peaches, cherries, clementines, whatever is her fruit of choice—usually from a local farm stand—can easily be fashioned into an arrangement using a decorative bowl filled with lemon leaves. There are no rules. "I just use what I'm attracted to," she says. If turnips are in season, she may arrange them just as prominently on her sideboard as a vase of tree peonies. The lack of rigidity in her designs reflects a well-balanced dance between the thoughtfully composed and the unconventionally splendid.

For Cathy, there are so many ways to employ flowers, including using them as a means of "redecorating" her house. "I don't change anything," she says. "Not even a pillow, and if I do, I re-cover it in the same fabric." What she does change, however, constantly and enthusiastically, are the flowers, which can "set the tone or mood that I want to create." Her townhouse, designed in collaboration with the brilliant decorator

William Hodgins, can be transformed from a calming and elegant domain into a show-stopping, fun-filled abode with splashes of exuberantly colored blossoms, unruly vines, and fragrant citrus fruits, along with charming miniature collectibles, inconspicuously placed on every surface imaginable. And nothing reflects Cathy's ability to reimagine a space more than when she entertains.

When she's hosting—and she has dinner parties throughout the year—she delves into every detail from start to finish. And when the time comes for her to plan an occasion, a creative collision between her sophisticated and whimsical tendencies occurs in the most instinctive way.

An important consideration for every table arrangement is the size and scale of the flowers: some settings call for individual stems in glass bottles for a translucent effect, others for groupings of various cut blooms, and still others for one generously sized, dramatic, and awe-inspiring centerpiece.

hen there are the table linens, for which Cathy has only one rule: they can never overshadow the floral arrangements. She gravitates toward seasonal colors and feels that one can never go wrong with white, pale green, pastel yellow, vibrant turquoise, tiny gingham checks, or wide stripes.

The selection of the components for her table arrangements is the result of mixing and matching and a bit of trial and error, right down to deciding which of her quirky collection of miniatures to include. The late great gossip columnist and party planner Elsa Maxwell, who had a penchant for sending her guests on scavenger hunts, once said, "Serve the dinner backward, do anything—but for goodness sake, do something weird." Although Cathy doesn't make anyone go on a wild goose chase, she does infuse a good dose of whimsy into her décor.

Doll-sized furniture, vintage toy bottles of Milk of Magnesia, miniature celluloid farm animals, countertop mannequins, and a toy New York City sanitation truck—most found on eBay—have all made appearances on Cathy's tables. "I like to mix in a little bad taste," she says, to the relief of any guest, particularly those who may be uptight or new to the group. Like the interior decorator Dorothy Draper once said, "I always put in one controversial item. It makes people talk." And very few topics get the chatter flowing faster than when Cathy places a miniature toy can of roach killer next to someone's glass of wine.

For any party, invitations must be sent. And Cathy always sets the tone for an event with her signature invites and reminder cards. Deriving inspiration from her favorite design period, the 1920s–1950s, she'll create a watercolor around the theme of the affair, incorporating some of her favorite motifs—cherries, x's, irises, or camellias—and embellish the design with German glass glitter, vintage stamps, or glued-on beads to add dimension. The result is always personal and eclectic, a testament to her desire to present her friends with artistic keepsakes on celebratory occasions.

Her Christmas cards are legendary and considered gifts in and of themselves. Nothing kicks off the season jollier than receiving one of Cathy's delightful and sparkly 7-by-9-inch watercolor treasures outfitted with cutout wrapping paper, gift tags, and painted holly.

Similar to the many different ways Cathy employs flowers, her use of watercolor extends well beyond wall hangings and cards. A day at the market can be the inspiration for painted candle shades, perfect for ambient lighting on the table or the mantel. Or for covering votive candle holders with watercolor images of flowers, stars, or, at Christmastime, sprigs of evergreen and berries, to cast a colorful glow on the table. Whether notebooks, gift boxes, or sets of cards with envelopes, Cathy's watercolors and illustrations add that layer of ingenuity that friends and family have come to expect, anticipate, and love.

In her work, Cathy isn't afraid to mix the refined with the raw, the traditional with the eccentric. What's most important to her is the feeling of contentment when she's creating, and the enjoyment she feels when she shares her artistry with those around her.

For Cathy, it's absolutely fine to mix pressed-glass vases with crystal stemware and place ceramic containers next to heirloom china. Or to have a watercolor of stunning botanicals share the page with painted ladies' gloves and bunches of cherries. Her playfully feminine and eclectic style radiates through everything she touches.

Cathy's *Second Bloom* is filled with endless ideas. "I feel very much like I did when I was in my twenties. I have more time to devote to my art and that fills me with such satisfaction," she says. And for those in their second chapter, or frankly, for anyone passionate about flowers and beautifying spaces, it starts with a love of creativity—something Cathy Graham has in unlimited supply for every season and every occasion.

"Nothing is so beautiful as spring— when weeds, in wheels, shoot long and lovely and lush..." —*Gerard Manley Hopkins*

Bursts of corals, pinks, oranges, and yellows, in hues ranging from soft to intense, are among Cathy's favorite color stories for her spring creations. But more than anything, whatever flowers, fruits, and vegetables are in season and catch her eye are the ones she chooses.

She carefully considers colors, textures, and varieties for all her flower arrangements. For extravagant spring centerpieces—whether for the table, mantel, or foyer—she loves to mix augmented blooms like camellias, peonies, dahlias, and garden roses with smaller varietals such as pansies, geraniums, and violets, mostly in different tones of similar colors, like pinks and lavenders, for added depth and dimension. Channeling Constance Spry, Cathy includes touches of curly willow and vines for an unexpected infusion of unruliness.

Of course there are occasions that call for a less traditional look. Cathy frequently makes arrangements for luncheon parties or even for her own dressing table that she calls "still lifes"—single stems of blousy blossoms like tulips, peonies, roses, and poppies placed in individual vintage glass bottles—usually purchased on eBay—for a translucent feel. This type of design not only allows guests to see each other easily across the table without obstruction, but also lets Cathy play with different heights for added interest. And hanging vines or ladies' gloves from the ceiling isn't out of the realm of possibility for some of her settings either.

The most important aspect of her flower arrangements, regardless of the shape, proportion, or tone, is that Cathy's playful spirit shines through. And her penchant for sprinkling miniature trinkets on her tabletops, even for the most formal of occasions, evokes a whimsical and joyous feeling.

Whatever varietals Cathy falls in love with while she's roaming around the flower markets will be displayed beautifully, thoughtfully, and eclectically. As Claude Monet said, "I must have flowers, always and always." Cathy wouldn't have it any other way.

Cathy sketches in her sunlit studio seven days a week. For her watercolors, she uses Schmincke paint with Winsor & Newton sable brushes, and she draws with Prismacolor colored pencils, all of which she finds at Utrecht Art Supplies, Blick Art Materials, or Artist & Craftsman Supply in Harlem. A bulletin board is covered with her fashion illustrations inspired by couture shows, her watercolor of tastemaker and friend Deeda Blair, and her favorite illustration by Kenneth Paul Block of a voluminous, strapless, floral-print dress.

GERTRUDe
STEIN

BaLMAIN

MADAM

BASKet

HATs
ot the DRy Clea

The mantel in Cathy's studio is a perfect illustration of her feminine, elegant, and whimsical aesthetic. Items include Livia Cetti's hand-dyed tissue paper flowers from John Derian, displayed in Cathy's vintage glass bottles from eBay and Pier 1 Imports; her favorite mannequin head from an antiques fair; mercury-glass vases given to her by the late event planner Robert Isabell; and a skull for anatomical drawings.

A close-up of a Coral Charm peony, one of Cathy's favorite flowers. In a niche painted celery green in the living room of her New York townhouse, she places cut tulips, ranunculus, fritillaria, and peonies in individual vases near antique creamware plates, to create the effect of having botanical plates. Bowls of fresh lemons and peaches are decorated with lemon leaves, which are sold in most flower shops.

For the table, I like to put individual flowers in my vintage bottles.

For an invitation that Cathy made for her friend Patty Dryden's birthday party, she started with a vintage paper doll she found on eBay, glued a photo of Dryden's face on it, and decorated it with a conical hat inspired by a 1940 Chesterfield ad, a skirt made of iridescent cellophane, glittered tulle, feathers, and a pink velvet bow. Stick-ons, including bobble eyes, star earrings, a crepe paper collar, and pearl beads added dimension and touches of whimsy.

Cathy hosted a dinner party for Amanda Foreman in honor of the premiere of her BBC series *The Ascent of Women*. She dressed the table with Royal Copenhagen china and ribbed, octagonal-shaped Murano glassware. Cut stems of tulips, roses, sweet peas, English daisies, and lilacs were displayed in glass bottles for that gleaming and transparent look she enjoys creating. Eclectic trinkets included a miniature ice truck, a sanitation truck, and antique European figurines of animal musicians.

40

HOW TO CREATE A "STILL LIFE" FOR THE TABLE

One of Cathy's signature table arrangements is a "still-life." The design is achieved by placing individual cut flowers in their own translucent bottles to create an ethereal look. Here, she primarily uses peonies, garden roses, tulips, carnations, ranunculus, and pansies.

1. Amass a collection of glass bottles in different sizes. Cathy prefers glass that is clear, pale blue, aqua, or pale green. She finds most of her bottles, such as her early twentieth-century pharmaceutical bottles, on eBay.

2. Choose a variety of flowers that differ in height, texture, and color intensity.

3. Pluck or use garden shears to remove leaves from the part of the stem that fits inside the bottle.

4. Cut the flowers at different heights to add dimension to the table. Each cut should be at a 45-degree angle so the blooms can absorb water more easily.

5. Place each flower in its own bottle.

6. Arrange the bottles in an appealing way.

45

I love
bringing potted
plants outside
in spring.

Cathy stands in the doorway of her Upper East Side townhouse, where she prefers to fill the window boxes with only one type of flower but create an explosion of different blooms in the garden.

Vibrant cut flowers, fruit, and fresh herbs, individually placed in an assortment of glass bottles and dishes, are displayed on the Art Deco mirrored commode in the front hall. The array of tree peonies, nasturtiums, Gloriosa lilies, roses, clematis, lilacs, petunias, sweet peas, sage, thyme, thistle, dianthus, and cherries creates a cheerful welcome for visitors.

When Cathy hosted a party for Flora Fraser to celebrate the publication of her book *Princesses: The Six Daughters of George III*, she used the theme of the book as inspiration. For the three-dimensional invitation, she painted a watercolor of six aristocratic women and embellished the print with pink feathers, ribbons, and beads.

Tones of pink and coral are among Cathy's favorite color combinations, as seen in this bouquet of clematis, sweet peas, garden roses, peonies, lilacs, and ranunculus. Beneath her set of Cy Twombly's *Some Trees of Italy* prints (1976), she decorates her George III satinwood and mahogany sideboard with white hydrangea plants, maidenhair ferns, pressed-glass bowls filled with clementines, a ceramic bowl of lemons, ceramic fig leaves from John Derian, bubbled-shaped antique glass paperweights, and a countertop mannequin doll.

An explosion of spring blossoms that Cathy found at the market inspired her to create a lavish arrangement for her dining room table. She chose a celery-and-cream-striped silk tablecloth to anchor the display of garden roses, peonies, geraniums, petunias, cherries, strawberries, and passion flowers in hues of pink, lavender, and coral. Peapods are scattered about the table.

62

"I wonder what it would be like
to live in a world where
it was always June." —*Lucy Maud Montgomery*

Gardening has been a passion of Cathy's ever since she was a child and learned about flowers from her maternal grandmother. Today, despite her aversion to worms, she spends a good part of the summer tending her cutting garden in Nantucket. Earlier in the year, she peruses the garden catalogues and makes the rounds of the nurseries to choose the flowers she wants to plant. Her selection is based on the arrangements she plans to create and the blooms she wishes to paint.

When it comes to entertaining, alfresco dining with a view of Nantucket Sound is one of the great pleasures that the summer house offers, but she often creates an ethereal feeling for indoor occasions as well. For her centerpieces, she may use peaches and cherries in lieu of flowers, showing the versatility of decorating with seasonal produce. Or she may create one of her favorite "still lifes," featuring delicate arrangements of cut flowers placed individually in glass bottles. And of course, she incorporates her quirky miniature collectibles into every design.

It goes without saying that Cathy spends hours painting watercolors in her studio with its views of Nantucket Sound. What better way to spend a summer afternoon than creating romantic botanicals on paper or on candle shades and votive holders, all of which are part of her artistic repertoire?

Henry James once said, "Summer afternoon—summer afternoon; to me those have always been the two most beautiful words in the English language." And Cathy's Nantucket home, adorned with the stunning flowers from her garden, is one of the most beautiful places to be in summer, no matter the time of day.

New Dawn climbing roses cover the side of
the shingled playhouse, a favorite destination
for Cathy's children when they were young.
Surrounding the exterior of the main house are
hydrangeas in blues, whites, and lavenders.

*First thing in
the morning
I prune roses,
cut flowers, and
condition them.*

Cathy likes to collect seashells on the beach or purchase them at little shops around town, displaying them in light wicker baskets. A spray rose in a clear bottle is pretty enough on its own.

Garden roses are in abundance inside and around Cathy's Nantucket house. Bouquets of garden roses in hues of pink add a pop of color against a mostly pale interior. New Dawn climbing roses adorn the wooden fence that surrounds the cutting garden.

In the dining room, Cathy arranges a
multicolored still life on the sideboard using
foxgloves, garden roses, passion flower
vines, and dianthus. For the centerpiece,
she creates a luxuriant bouquet of
hydrangeas in tones of pink, lavender, and
blue with a sprinkling of peach foxgloves.

Hand-blown glasses in shades of blue, green, and lavender hold Cathy's colored pencils for whenever she gets the urge to sketch. They also make perfect containers for bouquets. Here, she combined phlox, garden roses, and dahlias.

Cathy's miniature treasures are scattered among single stems of flowers on the dressing table in the first-floor powder room. Celluloid farm animals, a pair of polar bears, miniature bathroom fixtures, and even a miniature mop lend this still life a good dose of whimsy.

I enjoy painting paper candle shades with my favorite motifs for dinner parties.

A day in the cutting garden is the inspiration for many of
Cathy's watercolors of botanicals. For ambient lighting and a
touch of floral charm, she paints votive holders in watercolor.

A hollyhock in hot pink, one of Cathy's favorite colors for summer flowers. For an unrestrained, exuberant still life, she selects towering Sorbonne and Casablanca lilies, hollyhocks, dahlias, and sweet peas.

The flower room is
where Cathy creates her
arrangements. After cutting
the blooms in the morning,
she conditions them to
prolong their shelf life,
then lets them settle for a
few hours before arranging
them in a bouquet.

HOW TO CONDITION FLOWERS

To prolong the life of flowers, they must be properly conditioned first. There are universal steps that Cathy follows to keep her blossoms fresh as long as possible. One is to cut flowers first thing in morning when they're at their freshest and strongest.

1. Fill a bucket with room-temperature water a third of the way.

2. Remove any leaves from the stem that would end up underwater. Weak leaves can be plucked off. Use a sharp knife to remove tougher ones. Do not use a sawing motion, which could damage the stem.

3. Remove any thorns from the stem with either garden shears or a sharp knife.

4. Make a fresh cut at an angle one inch from the base of the stem using garden shears or a sharp knife. For flowers like poppies that bleed white milky juices, sear the end of the stem over a flame to seal the cut and preserve moisture.

5. Place each flower in the bucket as soon as you cut the stem.

6. Repeat this process until all the flowers have been conditioned.

7. Place the bucket in a cool place out of direct sunlight.

8. Let the flowers drink for several hours before arranging them in a bouquet.

9. Fill the bouquet container halfway with water and replenish it regularly, usually every two days.

10. Repeat the cutting process each time you replenish the water.

Cathy hosts dinners throughout the summer. Here, an aqua-and-white-checked gingham tablecloth is the linen of choice. Planned seating is her preference. "I think it's more special, plus people like to know where they sit," she says. She writes the names on all her place cards in her unique handwriting.

*In summer,
I often set my
table with an
arrangement
of fresh fruit.*

Wearing a floral-print Luisa Beccaria dress, Cathy hosts a summer luncheon for which the table decoration was inspired by fresh fruit.

For this alfresco luncheon, Cathy selected an aqua tablecloth set with antique plates and various pressed-glass bowls. The arrangements of lemons and peaches are accented with lemon leaves.

126

> "I trust in nature for the stable
> laws of beauty and utility.
> Spring shall plant and autumn garner
> to the end of time." —*Robert Browning*

Philosopher and writer Albert Camus said, "Autumn is a second spring when every leaf is a flower," an observation that Cathy embraces wholeheartedly. Come fall, she's back in her Manhattan townhouse, which means she's also back to weekly excursions to the Union Square Greenmarket and the Flower District to find luscious, colorful, and seasonal blossoms, fruits, and vegetables for inspiration and much more.

True to her eclectic taste, she gravitates toward whatever grabs her attention and looks stunning and stimulating. Eggplant, kale, cabbage, okra, peas, and radishes. These seasonal vegetables make delicious dishes, of course, but for Cathy they are also sublime adornments for her tabletops and floral arrangements. Keeping autumnal colors in mind, she may choose dahlias, poppies, hydrangeas, tuberoses, and zinnias—all seasonal flowers—and mix them with curly willow branches and fresh herbs, like thyme and rosemary.

For Cathy, the drop in temperature inspires countless new ways to decorate. On a chilly evening, what better way to enhance a roaring fire than to create an extravagant floral arrangement on the mantel above it? In her library, she takes advantage of the mantel's height and width to compose displays of blooms and vines that soar toward the ceiling and spill over the surface. Inspired by the paintings of Victorian artist Richard Dadd, whose best-known works were created when he was in Bedlam, they're beautiful, wild, utterly mad, and, memorable.

For a an early fall luncheon in the back garden of her townhouse, Cathy creates a table setting using only vegetables in a pattern inspired by the eighteenth-century silk textile designs of such artists as Anna Maria Garthwaite and James Leman.

HOW TO DECORATE WITH VEGETABLES

Choose seasonal, vibrantly colored vegetables that vary in size. Here Cathy chose peapods, radishes, baby eggplants, Brussels sprouts, gherkins, and okra.

1. Wash and clean the vegetables in cold water and let them dry completely.

2. Prep the vegetables for presentation. For the okra, for instance, Cathy sliced it thinly to form flower-shaped rounds.

3. Map out the design right on the tablecloth.

4. Put wax paper templates underneath any vegetables that could stain.

5. Simulate the shape of long-stemmed flowers by using herbs such as chives as stems.

6. Create motifs. Here Cathy created a pinwheel pattern out of peapods.

7. Use glue dots on the back of vegetables to keep them from moving.

8. Introduce pops of color for contrast. Here Cathy used baby eggplants to offset the green leaves, okra, gherkins, and peas.

Inspired by the textures, shapes, and bold colors of fresh seasonal vegetables, Cathy paints them in watercolor.

I use herbs in my arrangements to create fragrant bouquets.

For a luncheon in the back garden of her townhouse, Cathy chooses navy-blue-and-white pillows in a bold print to contrast with the table setting's celery and white palette. A lavish centerpiece of zinnias, peonies, garden roses, dahlias, lavender, sage, and thyme adds a dramatic infusion of color, texture, and aroma.

144

The blousy Coral Charm peony with its yellow stamen fades to a soft apricot pink as it matures. Here, the Coral Charm is incorporated into a bouquet of garden roses, lavender, zinnias, and ranunculus.

Paper stores are a great source of inspiration.

For her reminder cards, Cathy prefers collages incorporating vintage graphics, stickers, and old recipe pamphlets. She sometimes uses embossed foil Dresden trim as a border.

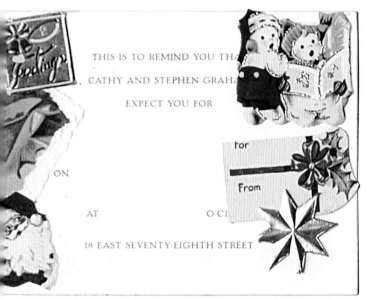

THIS IS TO REMIND YOU THAT

CATHY AND STEPHEN GRAHAM

EXPECT YOU FOR

for

From

ON

AT   O'CLOCK

18 EAST SEVENTY-EIGHTH STREET

Jell-O Rules

HAPPINESS!

A MESSAGE FOR YOU

JELL-O

Frankfurter Scallop

THIS IS TO REMIND

CATHY AND STEPHEN

EXPECT YOU

dinner

APRIL 4+

AT   8:00   O'CLOCK

18 EAST SEVENTY-EIGHTH ST

1928
Sealed with
Rhubarb
Good Luck Rubbers

PEAR
DATE

24 VELVETY FLOCKED 10c
MEDIUM
SEALS
PECK 200

PEAR
DATE Lu 7

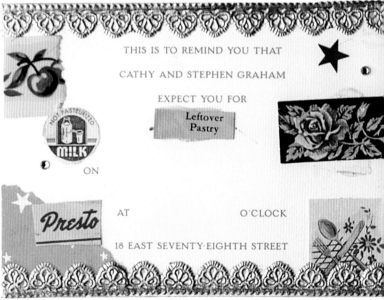

THIS IS TO REMIND YOU THAT

CATHY AND STEPHEN GRAHAM

EXPECT YOU FOR

Leftover
Pastry

ON

MILK

Presto

AT   O'CLOCK

18 EAST SEVENTY-EIGHTH STREET

I always look for flowers with personality.

Using fall colors like burgundy and aubergine, Cathy combines Sorbonne lilies, passion flower vines, dahlias, and clematis with Queen Anne's lace, berries, grasses, and eucalyptus to create a massive arrangement that spills over her front hall table.

Inspired by nineteenth-century painter Richard Dadd, Cathy creates mammoth arrangements on the mantel in her library, where she's free to play with height and width.

On the living room mantel, Cathy creates an arrangement inspired by the bare twigs and branches indicative of fall. Eucalyptus, stalks of wheat, roots, twigs, garden roses, dahlias, zinnias, hydrangeas, pods, and bachelor buttons fill one of her favorite metal planters.

HOW TO CREATE A FLORAL ARRANGEMENT

1. Sort your conditioned stems by color and size.

2. Select the container. Here Cathy chooses a large metal planter.

3. Soak Oasis floral foam in water, then cut to fit the base of the container.

4. Start by placing greenery to shape the structure of the arrangement, focusing on height and width.

5. Work in a symmetrical fashion so that whatever is introduced on one side of the container is balanced on the other.

6. Make sure that the ratio of the container to the flowers is proportional. Ideally, the container should be 1/3 of the total arrangement; the flowers, 2/3.

171

"What good is the warmth of summer,
without the cold of winter
to give it sweetness." —*John Steinbeck*

When the holiday season rolls around, Cathy goes into high gear. In her townhouse, the iconic elements are all there—garlands, ornaments, and, naturally, flowers. But instead of décor that screams and shouts Christmas, her aesthetic incorporates thoughtful selections that always surprise and delight.

In lieu of a garland adorned with the predictable pine cones, red velvet ribbons, large ornaments, and holiday berries, Cathy might opt for sugarcoated fruit ornaments, variegated holly, cherries, vines, and just a few celluloid reindeer sprinkled in for a hint of Christmas. Rather than a large bouquet of poinsettias, she fills vases with pink garden roses and camellias. And a setting wouldn't be complete without her eccentric miniatures or her watercolor candle shades.

Cathy's Christmas cards are works of art—watercolors embellished with German glass glitter, beads, or marabou feathers and a collage of her favorite motifs. She's been making cards for years, to the delight of friends who receive the 7-by-9-inch envelopes in the mail or delivered by hand.

Winter is the season to be jolly. And the colorful and original aesthetic that Cathy infuses into every floral arrangement, table setting, card, and party favor guarantees a happy holiday for one and all.

For a cocktail party Cathy hosted in honor of her dear friend the costume designer William Ivey Long, her invitation featured a watercolor portrait of him, embellished with feathers, stars, and miniature whiskey bottles. She also glued on cutouts of leading actors from the Broadway musicals for which Long had designed the costumes, including Anita Morris in *Nine* and Alan Cumming in *Cabaret*.

For the front hall table, Cathy created a Constance Spry–inspired arrangement with camellias, Majolica spray roses, variegated and antique roses in different tones of mauve, curly willow, pastel flowering kale, white winter berries, and cabbages on the stem. A card illustrated with costume sketches by Long and Barbie dolls lying in less-than-ladylike positions added those touches of the unexpected for which Cathy is renowned. A doll attired in the famous Chrysler Building dress from *The Producers* adorned the mantel. In the living room, she hung stars and the letters of Long's name, covered in German glass glitter, from the ceiling using monofilament fishing line.

There's nothing like a handmade Christmas card.

For Jane Stubbs and Emily Eerdman's Christmas show in Greenwich Village, Cathy made some of her signature watercolor Christmas cards. For one, she created Santa's beard out of a cotton ball. Gift boxes embellished with her witty three-dimensional collages make perfect receptacles not only for stationery but also for her grandmother's Viennese crescent cookies, which she gives as party favors. Round boxes hold her watercolor candle shades.

For a holiday dinner party, Cathy opted for a palette of turquoise and deep pinks, instead of the more traditional red and green. She covered the table with a deep turquoise satin tablecloth strewn with swatches of glittered tulle and set it with Ralph Lauren crystal wine glasses and Richard Ginori dinner plates. On top of each plate, she placed a favor box ornamented with a three-dimensional collage. To complete the festive look, she created an arrangement of ranunculus, sweet peas, tulips, amaryllis, roses, anemones, clementines, and cranberries that ran the length of the table. Interspersed among the flowers and fruit were her quirky collectibles, including sugarcoated fruit ornaments, celluloid reindeer, spun-cotton elf ornaments, a red fedora, a doll-sized Jr. Mixer "whipping up" frothy pink marabou, a Ken doll wrapped in fur, a vintage Bromo-Seltzer bottle, and an antique toy airplane resting atop a cake stand.

A festive holiday garland draping the mirror in the front hallway sets the tone for one of Cathy's Christmas parties. It is ornamented with cherries, garden roses, pink hydrangeas, asparagus ferns, camellia leaves, variegated holly, lamb's ears, berries, peonies, and herbs. Bouquets of tulips, sweet peas, ranunculus, and garden roses share the table with a selection of her miniature collectibles, including a Milk of Magnesia bottle, toy sanitation and ice trucks, celluloid reindeer, a cake plate with a fake martini, a doll-sized toilet, and a countertop mannequin head wearing one of her watercolor candle shades. Vintage countertop mannequins finish off the quirky and colorful display.

198

HOW TO MAKE A FESTIVE GARLAND

Cathy uses garlands to decorate her front hall mirror and the French doors leading to her living room. She mixes sugarcoated fruit ornaments and fresh fruit with iconic Christmas elements like candy canes and German glass glitter stars.

1. Sort the decorative items by category. Here Cathy made separate piles of candy canes, apples, celluloid reindeer, German glass glitter stars, vintage fruit ornaments, and real apples and clementines.

2. Create mini bouquets by tying together a variety of items with floral wire.

3. Secure the garland above the doorframe. Heavy garlands may need to be reinforced with wire and nails. Here Cathy intertwined two evergreen garlands to create one thick garland.

4. Attach the mini bouquets to the garland with more wire.

5. Complete the garland by attaching stars, candy canes, and reindeer directly to it.

Sources

ART/PAPER SUPPLIES
Artist & Craftsman Supply
artistcraftsman.com

Bell'occhio
bellocchio.com

Blick Art Materials
dickblick.com

Create
nantucketcreate.com

JAM Paper
jampaper.com

Michaels
michaels.com

Paper Presentation
paperpresentation.com

Parchment Fine Papers
parchmentnantucket.com

COLLECTIBLES
Bizarre Bazaar
bzrbzr.com

eBay
ebay.com

Etsy
etsy.com

Ruby Lane
rubylane.com

Tail of the Yak Trading Company
(510) 841-9891

Theatre of Dreams
wendyaddisonstudio.com

Tinsel Trading
tinseltrading.com

FABRICS
Bennison
bennisonfabrics.com

Chelsea Editions
chelseatextiles.com

Colefax and Fowler
cowtan.com/colefax-and-fowler

Lee Jofa
leejofa.com

Mood Fabrics
moodfabrics.com

Quadrille
quadrillefabrics.com

FARM PRODUCE
Dutch Flower Line
dutchflowerline.com

Flowers on Chestnut
flowersonchestnut.com

Foliage Garden
foliagegarden.com

G. Page Wholesale Flowers
gpage.com

J Rose Wholesale Flowers
jrosewholesaleflowers.com

Persuad (Twenty Eight Street
Wholesale Flowers)
(212) 967-5610

Surfing Hydrangea
surfinghydrangea.com

Union Square Greenmarket
grownyc.org/greenmarket/manhattan-
union-square-m

HOME FURNISHINGS
ABC Carpet & Home
aABC Carpet & Home
abchome.com

Baccarat
us.baccarat.com

Bardith
bardith.com

Bodega
bodeganantucket.com

Carmen Almon
carmenalmon.com

Christofle
christofle.com/us_en

Coastal Nantucket
coastalnantucket.com

Hollyhock
hollyhockinc.com

John Derian
johnderian.com

Just Shades
justlampshades.com

Lars Bolander
larsbolander.com

The Lion's Paw
thelionspawnantucket.net

Mud Australia
mudaustralia.com

Nantucket Looms
nantucketlooms.com

Neue Gallery
neuegalerie.org

Ralph Lauren Home
ralphlaurenhome.com

Rose Tarlow
rosetarlow.com

Sue Fisher King
suefisherking.com

Vladimir Kanevsky
thevladimircollection.com

Weatherend Furniture
weatherend.com

LINENS
Casa Del Bianco
casadelbianco.com

D. Porthault
dporthaultparis.com

Fine Linens
finelinens.com

Nancy Stanley Waud Fine Linens
(310) 273-3690

MISCELLANEOUS (HOME DECOR/
JEWELRY/FASHION ACCESSORIES)
Elements
elementschicago.com

Acknowledgments

First of all, I want to thank Howard Slatkin for his faith and encouragement throughout the twenty years of our friendship. This book never would have happened without his unswerving support and belief in me. Thanks also to Deeda Blair, who is an inspiration and has the most exquisite eye, and to William Ivey Long, the brilliant costume designer, a supportive friend during my darkest days. His creativity astounds and inspires me.

I owe a great debt of gratitude to my dear friend Joanna Coles, who insisted I post daily on Instagram and wrote the wonderful Foreword. I am also deeply indebted to my supportive friends who have always tried to push me to break out of my inertia and show my work: Anne Kramer, James Lapine, Jorie Graham, and Peter Sacks. Boundless thanks to Mark and Nina Magowan for taking the leap of faith to publish this book and to Jill Cohen for bringing in designer Doug Turshen and photographers Quentin Bacon and Andy Ingalls, whom I can't thank enough for their beautiful work and their patience dealing with a novice. Thanks as well to author Alexis Clark and editor Jacqueline Decter for helping me to express what I strive to do. To Ellice Grande and Philippa Brathwaite for their help in styling some of the photo shoots. To Michael Fullwood, Liz Garvin, and Thomas Boucher from my Robert Isabell days, who were instrumental in helping me create the William Ivey Long party. To Lisa Currie and Luz Valencia for their immeasurable help in everything I do. To Valrie Riddick, who has made the trains run on time. To digital wizard Floor van de Velde for all of her assistance. And to my wonderful, creative children, Tommy and Juliet.

—Cathy Graham

First published in the United States of America by
The Vendome Press
www.vendomepress.com
Vendome is a registered trademark of The Vendome Press, LLC

ISBN 978-0-86565-343-6

Editor: Jacqueline Decter
Production Director: Jim Spivey
Production Color Manager: Dana Cole
Designers: Doug Turshen with David Huang

Developed in conjunction with Jill Cohen Associates
Front cover photo styled by Philippa Brathwaite

Library of Congress Cataloging-in-Publication Data
Names: Clark, Alexis, author.
Title: Second bloom : Cathy Graham's art of the table / by Alexis Clark ;
  foreword by Joanna Coles ; photography by Quentin Bacon and Andrew Ingalls.
Description: New York : Vendome, [2017]
Identifiers: LCCN 2017016336 | ISBN 9780865653436 (acid-free paper)
Subjects: LCSH: Table setting and decoration. | Entertaining. | Graham, Cathy.
Classification: LCC TX879 .C55 2017 | DDC 642/.4--dc23
LC record available at https://lccn.loc.gov/2017016336

This book was produced using acid-free paper, processed
chlorine free, and printed with soy-based inks.

Printed in China by OGI
First printing